KEEP CALM YOU'RE ONLY 50   KEEP CALM YOU'RE ONLY 50   KEEP CALM YOU'RE ONLY 50   KEEP CALM YOU'RE ONLY 50

KEEP CALM YOU'RE ONLY 50   KEEP CALM YOU'RE ONLY 50   KEEP CALM YOU'RE ONLY 50   KEEP CALM YOU'RE ONLY 50

KEEP CALM YOU'RE ONLY 50   KEEP CALM YOU'RE ONLY 50   KEEP CALM YOU'RE ONLY 50   KEEP CALM YOU'RE ONLY 50

KEEP CALM YOU'RE ONLY 50   KEEP CALM YOU'RE ONLY 50   KEEP CALM YOU'RE ONLY 50   KEEP CALM YOU'RE ONLY 50

KEEP CALM

YOU'RE ONLY

50

KEEP CALM YOU'RE ONLY 50

Summersdale Publishers Ltd
46 West Street
Chichester
West Sussex
PO19 1RP
UK

www.summersdale.com

Printed and bound in the Czech Republic

ISBN: 978-1-84953-223-5

Substantial discounts on bulk quantities of Summersdale books are available to corporations, professional associations and other organisations. For details contact Summersdale Publishers by telephone: +44 (0) 1243 771107, fax: +44 (0) 1243 786300 or email: nicky@summersdale.com.

KEEP
CALM

YOU'RE ONLY

50

summersdale

CONTENTS

ANOTHER
YEAR
OLDER

Happy 20th anniversary of your 30th Birthday!

Anonymous

It takes a long time to become young.

Pablo Picasso

By the time we hit 50…
we have learned to take
life seriously, but never
ourselves.

Marie Dressler

As a graduate of the Zsa Zsa Gabor School of Creative Mathematics, I honestly do not know how old I am.

Erma Bombeck

We're vintage!

Jennifer Saunders and
Dawn French on both reaching 50

Forty is the old age of youth;
50 the youth of old age.

Victor Hugo

To me, old age is always 15 years older than I am.

Bernard M. Baruch

About the only thing that
comes to us without effort
is old age.

Gloria Pitzer

I'd like to grow very old
as slowly as possible.

Charles Lamb

How old would you be
if you didn't know how
old you were?

Satchel Paige

The woman who tells her age is either too young to have anything to lose or too old to have anything to gain.

Chinese proverb

I refuse to admit I'm more than 52, even if that does make my sons illegitimate.

Nancy Astor

Few women admit
their age. Few men
act theirs.

Anonymous

No woman should ever be quite accurate about her age. It looks so calculating.

Oscar Wilde

For all the advances in medicine, there is still no cure for the common birthday.

John Glenn

In dog years, I'm dead.

Anonymous

Birthdays only come once a year unless you're Joan Collins, in which case they only come every four years.

Steve Bauer

JUST
WHAT
I
ALWAYS
WANTED

My present was a cake.
Ablaze with so many
candles, I fully expected
to see boy scouts camped
around it.

Anonymous

A friend never defends
a husband who gets
his wife an electric
skillet for her birthday.

Erma Bombeck

Yesterday is history,
tomorrow is a mystery, but
today is a gift. That is why it
is called the present.

Eleanor Roosevelt

A hug is the perfect gift;
one size fits all, and nobody
minds if you exchange it.

Anonymous

A gift, with a kind
countenance, is a
double present.

Thomas Fuller

At my age flowers
scare me.

George Burns

Age is just a number. It's totally irrelevant unless, of course, you happen to be a bottle of wine.

Joan Collins

A true friend
remembers your
birthday but not
your age.

Anonymous

Handmade presents are
scary because they reveal
that you have too much
free time.

Douglas Coupland

Youth is the gift of nature, but age is a work of art.

Garson Kanin

At my age the best gift one can hope for is a continuing sense of humour. The ability to laugh, especially at ourselves, keeps the heart light and the mind young.

Anonymous

Birthdays are good for you. Statistics show that the people who have the most live the longest.

Larry Lorenzoni

There are 364 days when you might get un-birthday presents... and only *one* for birthday presents, you know.

Lewis Carroll,
Through the Looking Glass

We know we're getting old
when the only thing we want
for our birthday is not to be
reminded of it.

Anonymous

GRIN

AND

BEAR

IT

Whenever the talk turns to age, I say I am 49 plus VAT.

Lionel Blair

The years teach much
which the days
never knew.

Ralph Waldo Emerson

Age is something that
doesn't matter, unless
you are a cheese.

Billie Burke

Every time I think that I'm getting old, and gradually going to the grave, something else happens.

Elvis Presley

Another belief of mine: that everyone else my age is an adult, whereas I am merely in disguise.

Margaret Atwood

Ageing is not 'lost youth' but a new stage of opportunity and strength.

Betty Friedan

One of the best parts of growing older? You can flirt all you like since you've become harmless.

Liz Smith

Growing old is
mandatory; growing
up is optional.

Chili Davis

It is a mistake to regard age as a downhill grade toward dissolution. The reverse is true. As one grows older, one climbs with surprising strides.

George Sand

One of the many
things nobody ever
tells you about middle
age is that it's such
a nice change from
being young.

Dorothy Canfield Fisher

The longer I live
the more beautiful
life becomes.

Frank Lloyd Wright

I believe in loyalty; I think
when a woman reaches a
certain age she likes she
should stick to it.

Eva Gabor

If you find yourself 50 years old and you aren't doing what you love, then what's the point?

Jim Carrey

Zeal, n. A certain
nervous disorder
afflicting the young
and inexperienced.

Ambrose Bierce

Nice to be here? At my age
it's nice to be anywhere.

George Burns

DO
A LITTLE
DANCE
MAKE
A LITTLE
LOVE

Old people aren't exempt
from having fun and
dancing... and playing.

Liz Smith

I'll keep swivelling
my hips until they
need replacing.

Tom Jones

Middle age is having
a choice between two
temptations and choosing
the one that'll get you
home earlier.

Dan Bennett

It's sex, not youth,
that's wasted on
the young.

Janet Harris

The ageing process
has you firmly in its
grasp if you never get
the urge to throw
a snowball.

Doug Larson

You know you're knocking
on when you feel like the
morning-after-the-night-
before without having
been anywhere.

Anonymous

The young sow wild
oats. The old
grow sage.

Winston Churchill

There's a kind of confidence
that comes when you're in
your forties and fifties, and
men find that incredibly
attractive.

Peggy Northrop

I'm limitless as far as age is concerned... as long as he has a driver's licence.

Kim Cattrall on dating younger men

Old wood best to burn, old
wine to drink, old friends to
trust, and old authors
to read.

Francis Bacon

A man is a fool if
he drinks before he
reaches 50, and a
fool if he doesn't
drink afterward.

Frank Lloyd Wright

We've both hit 50, and we celebrate it. There is no doomy side to it... We're nearly grown-up now, but not quite.

Dawn French and Jennifer Saunders

I don't believe in ageing. I believe in forever altering one's aspect to the sun. Hence my optimism.

Virginia Woolf

If you think hitting 40
is liberating, wait till
you hit 50.

Michelle Pfeiffer

YOUNG
AT
HEART

I'm surprised that I'm 50…
I still feel like a kid.

Bruce Willis

I'm aiming by the time
I'm 50 to stop being
an adolescent.

Wendy Cope

You can't turn back
the clock but you can
wind it up again.

Bonnie Prudden

The old believe everything;
the middle-aged suspect
everything: the young
know everything.

Oscar Wilde

Children are a great
comfort in your old age
– and they help you
reach it faster, too.

Lionel Kauffman

A young man is
embarrassed to
question an older one.

Homer

Growing old is a bad habit
which a busy man has no
time to form.

André Maurois

When grace is joined
with wrinkles, it is
adorable. There is an
unspeakable dawn in
happy old age.

Victor Hugo

My mother is going to have to stop lying about her age because pretty soon I'm going to be older than she is.

Tripp Evans

With age comes the inner, the higher life. Who would be forever young, to dwell always in externals?

Elizabeth Cady Stanton

As is a tale, so is life: not how long it is, but how good it is, is what matters.

Seneca

A man is not old
as long as he is
seeking something.

Jean Rostand

To get back my youth I would do anything in the world, except take exercise, get up early, or be respectable.

Oscar Wilde

The great thing about getting older is that you don't lose all the other ages you've been.

Madeleine L'Engle

The more you complain, the longer God lets you live!

Anonymous

To keep the heart unwrinkled, to be hopeful, kindly, cheerful, reverent – that is to triumph over old age.

Thomas Bailey Aldrich

OLDER
AND
WISER?

None are so old
as those who have
outlived enthusiasm.

Henry David Thoreau

From 40 to 50 a man must
move upward, or the natural
falling off in the vigour
of life will carry him
rapidly downward.

Oliver Wendell Holmes Jr

Young men's minds are
always changeable,
but when an old man is
concerned in a matter, he
looks both before and after.

Homer

The best way to get
most husbands to
do something is to
suggest that perhaps
they're too old to do it.

Anne Bancroft

One of the signs of passing youth is the birth of a sense of fellowship with other human beings as we take our place among them.

Virginia Woolf

He's so old that when he orders a three-minute egg, they ask for the money up front.

Milton Berle

Old men are fond of giving good advice, to console themselves for being no longer in a position to give bad examples.

François de La Rochefoucauld

To know how to grow
old is the masterwork
of wisdom.

Henri-Frédéric Amiel

You are only young
once, but you can
be immature for
a lifetime.

John P. Grier

I have enjoyed greatly the second blooming... suddenly you find – at the age of 50, say – that a whole new life has opened before you.

Agatha Christie

Old age puts more wrinkles in our minds than on our faces.

Michel de Montaigne

Becoming a grandmother
is wonderful. One moment
you're just a mother. The
next you are all-wise
and prehistoric.

Pam Brown

The surprising thing
about young fools is
how many survive to
become old fools.

Doug Larson

Before you contradict an old man, my fair friend, you should endeavour to understand him.

George Santayana

No man is ever
old enough to
know better.

Holbrook Jackson

When I was a boy of 14,
my father was so ignorant
I could hardly stand to
have the old man around.
But when I got to 21, I was
astonished at how much he
had learned in seven years.

Mark Twain

LIVE
LOVE
AND
LAST

He who laughs, lasts!

Mary Pettibone Poole

Tomorrow's gone – we'll have tonight!

Dorothy Parker

To stop ageing, keep on raging.

Michael Forbes

No matter how old you are, there's always something good to look forward to.

Lynn Johnston

The other day a man asked
me what I thought was the
best time of life. 'Why,' I
answered… 'now.'

David Grayson

The follies which a man
regrets most in his life
are those which he didn't
commit when he had
the opportunity.

Helen Rowland

Middle age is when
we can do just as
much as ever – but
would rather not.

Anonymous

Just remember, once you're over the hill you begin to pick up speed.

Charles M. Schulz

One can remain alive long past the usual date of disintegration if one is unafraid of change, insatiable in intellectual curiosity, interested in big things, and happy in small ways.

Edith Wharton

The time to begin
most things is ten
years ago.

Mignon McLaughlin

Nobody grows old merely by
living a number of years. We
grow old by deserting
our ideals.

Samuel Ullman

You can live to be a hundred
if you give up all the things
that make you want to live to
be a hundred.

Woody Allen

No man loves life like
him that's growing old.

Sophocles

The average child laughs about 400 times per day, the average adult laughs only 15 times per day. What happened to the other 385 laughs? Laugh and live!

Anonymous

The purpose of life is to fight maturity.

Dick Werthimer

May you live all the
days of your life.

Jonathan Swift

Age does not protect you from love. But love to some extent, protects you from age.

Jeanne Moreau

Time doth flit; oh shit!

Dorothy Parker

ILLS
PILLS
AND
TWINGES

Old age is no place for sissies.

Bette Davis

My doctor told me to do something that puts me out of breath, so I've taken up smoking again.

Jo Brand

You know you've reached
middle-age when your
weightlifting consists merely
of standing up.

Bob Hope

Middle age is when
you choose your
cereal for the fibre,
not the toy.

Anonymous

The years between 50 and 70 are the hardest. You are always being asked to do more, and you are not yet decrepit enough to turn them down.

T. S. Eliot

I would rather be round and jolly than thin and cross.

Ann Widdecombe

I feel stronger now than,
maybe, 20 years ago. If your
mind is strong, your body
will be strong.

Madonna

Middle age is the time
when a man is always
thinking in a week
or two he will feel as
good as ever.

Don Marquis

If I'd known I was
going to live this long,
I'd have taken better
care of myself.

Eubie Blake

I don't feel old. I don't feel anything till noon. That's when it's time for my nap.

Bob Hope

I never worry about diets. The only carrots that interest me are the number you get in a diamond.

Mae West

Old minds are like old horses; you must exercise them if you wish to keep them in working order.

John Quincy Adams

As you get older three things happen. The first is your memory goes, and I can't remember the other two...

Norman Wisdom

Age seldom arrives
smoothly or quickly.
It's more often a
succession of jerks.

Jean Rhys

What most persons consider
as virtue, after the age of 40
is simply a loss of energy.

Voltaire

People who say
you're just as old as
you feel are all wrong,
fortunately.

Russell Baker

You know you're getting old
when you stop to tie your
shoes and wonder what
else you can do while you're
down there.

George Burns

CHIN

UP

CHEST

OUT

You can only perceive
real beauty in a
person as they
get older.

Anouk Aimée

Middle age is when your age starts to show around your middle.

Bob Hope

The age of a woman doesn't mean a thing. The best tunes are played on the oldest fiddles.

Ralph Waldo Emerson

Grey hair is
God's graffiti.

Bill Cosby

I don't plan to grow old gracefully; I plan to have facelifts until my ears meet.

Rita Rudner

I was getting dressed and a
Peeping Tom looked in the
window… and pulled down
the shade.

Joan Rivers

Regrets are the
natural property of
grey hairs.

Charles Dickens

Please don't retouch my
wrinkles. It took me so long
to earn them.

Anna Magnani

When it comes to staying young, a mind-lift beats a facelift any day.

Marty Bucella

There is only one cure for grey hair. It was invented by a Frenchman. It is called the guillotine.

P. G. Wodehouse

I'm like old wine. They don't bring me out very often, but I'm well preserved.

Rose Kennedy

I'm not denying my age, I'm embellishing my youth.

Tamara Reynolds

Middle age is youth
without levity, and age
without decay.

Daniel Defoe

Nature gives you the face you have at 20, but it's up to you to merit the face you have at 50.

Coco Chanel

She was a handsome woman of 45 and would remain so for many years.

Anita Brookner

The secret of staying
young is to live
honestly, eat slowly
and lie about
your age.

Lucille Ball

KEEP
CALM
AND
DRINK
UP

KEEP CALM AND DRINK UP

£4.99

ISBN: 978 1 84953 102 3

'*In victory, you deserve champagne; in defeat, you need it.*'

Napoleon Bonaparte

BAD ADVICE FOR GOOD PEOPLE.

Keep Calm and Carry On, a World War Two government poster, struck a chord in recent difficult times when a stiff upper lip and optimistic energy were needed again. But in the long run it's a stiff drink and flowing spirits that keep us all going.

Here's a book packed with proverbs and quotations showing the wisdom to be found at the bottom of the glass.

www.summersdale.com